HRUBIAK, Emma

Working with gypsy/traveller
families to support literacy
development

NIACE lifelines in adult learning

The *NIACE lifelines in adult learning* series provides straightforward background and information, accessible know-how and useful examples of good practice for all practitioners involved in adult and community learning. Focusing in turn on different areas of adult learning these guides are an essential part of every practitioner's toolkit.

1. **Community education and neighbourhood renewal** – Jane Thompson, ISBN 978 1 86201 139 7
2. **Spreading the word: reaching out to new learners** – Veronica McGivney, ISBN 978 1 86201 140 3
3. **Managing community projects for change** – Jan Eldred, ISBN 978 1 86201 141 0
4. **Engaging black learners in adult and community education** – Lenford White, ISBN 978 1 86201 142 7
5. **Consulting adults** – Chris Jude, ISBN 978 1 86201 149 6
6. **Working with young adults** – Carol Jackson, ISBN 978 1 86201 150 2
7. **Promoting learning** – Kate Malone, ISBN 978 1 86201 151 9
8. **Evaluating community projects** – Jane Field, ISBN 978 1 86201 152 6
9. **Working in partnership** – Lyn Tett, ISBN 978 1 86201 162 5
10. **Working with Asian heritage communities** – David McNulty, ISBN 978 1 86201 174 8
11. **Learning and community arts** – Tony Fegan, ISBN 978 1 86201 181 6
12. **Museums and community learning** – Garrick Fincham, ISBN 978 1 86201 182 3
13. **Developing a needs-based library service** – John Pateman, ISBN 978 1 86201 183 0
14. **Volunteers and volunteering** – Janet Swinney, ISBN 978 1 86201 187 8
15. **Sustaining projects for success** – Kay Snowdon, ISBN 978 1 86201 188 5
16. **Opening up schools for adults** – Judith Summers, ISBN 978 1 86201 192 2
17. **Befriending learners** – Jane Field, ISBN 978 1 86201 210 3
18. **Developing literacy: supporting achievement** – Amanda Lindsay and Judith Gawn, ISBN 978 1 86201 216 5
19. **Developing numeracy: supporting achievement** – Barbara Newmarch, ISBN 978 1 86201 217 2
20. **Developing ESOL: supporting achievement** – Violet Windsor and Christina Healey, ISBN 978 1 86201 218 0
21. **Developing embedded literacy, language and numeracy: supporting achievement** – Jan Eldred, ISBN 978 1 86201 219 6
22. **Developing Literacy, Language and Numeracy in the Workplace** – Sue Southwood, ISBN 978 1 86201 247 9
23. **Supporting learners with dyslexia in workplace learning** – Rachel Davies and Heather Hardie, ISBN 978 1 86201 354 4
24. **Working with unions to develop literacy, language and numeracy in the workplace** – Sue Southwood and Judith Swift, ISBN 978 1 86201 355 1
    The Jargon Buster – Yanina Dutton, ISBN 978 1 86201 215 8

niace · lifelines in adult learning

25

Working with Gypsy/Traveller families to support literacy development

Emma Hrubiak

Published by the National Institute of
Adult Continuing Education (England and Wales)

21 De Montfort Street
Leicester LE1 7GE
Company registration no. 2603322
Charity registration no. 1002775

First published 2009

niace
promoting adult learning

NIACE has a broad remit to promote lifelong learning
opportunities for adults. NIACE works to develop
increased participation in education and training,
particularly for those who do not have easy access
because of barriers of class, gender, age, race,
language and culture, learning difficulties and
disabilities, or insufficient financial resources.

www.niace.org.uk

Cataloguing in Publication Data
A CIP record of this title is available from the British Library

Designed and typeset by Boldface, London
Printed in Great Britain by Russell Press, Nottingham
All photographs © Read On – Write Away! except pages viii and 2, courtesy of Liverpool University

ISBN 978 1 86201 374 2

Contents

Note to the reader

Inspirations: refer to case studies and examples of good practice.

Acknowledgements

Thanks for their contribution to this guide must go to:

Geoff Bright, Connexions
Mick Gough, Read On – Write Away!
Nigel Groom, Derbyshire and Derby City Traveller Education Advisory and Support Team
Annette Lowe, Read On – Write Away!
Teresa Lynch, crèche worker
Muzelley McCready, Derbyshire Gypsy Liaison Group
Jayne Morton, Skills for Life tutor
Pat Poxon, Read On – Write Away!
Lynne Ramsden, public health practitioner
Sarah Smith, family learning teacher, Read On – Write Away!
Siobhan Spencer, Derbyshire Gypsy Liaison Group
Jan Thompson, Derbyshire and Derby City Traveller Education Advisory and Support Team

Thanks also to all the families who have participated in the project and allowed us to use their photographs and stories.

Showman's wagon. Brough, Westmorland (Cumbria), 1911

Introduction

This Lifeline has been written for practitioners and managers in adult, community and family learning settings. It will also provide valuable insight for professionals working in other areas, for example health services. Although primarily for those with little or no experience of working with the Gypsy/Traveller community and cultures, the book will also be of interest to practitioners who work with these communities already as it describes the development of a successful family learning model that engages with, and benefits, all family members, adults and children alike.

It must be emphasised right at the start that this is the story of *Read On – Write Away!*, their partners and their journey together in working with Gypsy/Traveller families in Derbyshire; there are many successful projects around the country led by a variety of voluntary, community and statutory organisations who would be just as qualified, if not more so, to share their good practice. Equally, many schools have developed exemplary work with Gypsy/Traveller children and their families (DCSF, 2008). Links to some of these projects are provided at the end of this book.

The book aims to give professionals a brief insight into, and understanding of, the Gypsy/Traveller cultures. However, as with any other culture, these change and will continue to develop over time. It is important to say that the customs, values and traditions described in this book may not represent those of every Gypsy/Traveller. There is diversity within all groups.

As a practitioner, you may have been asked to begin work with a Gypsy/Traveller community, you may have an interest in Gypsy/Traveller cultures and communities or you may be looking to include Gypsy/Traveller communities in programmes that you already run. Whatever the reason you have chosen to read this guide, we hope that it will help answer some of your concerns and queries, break down barriers and remove myths. We hope that you will be inspired and will see a way that you too can engage and develop a healthy and beneficial professional relationship with the Gypsy/Traveller communities in your area.

PHOTOGRAPHER: FRED SHAW

Reading wagon with children seated on the steps. Barnet, Herts., 1921

1 Who are the Gypsy/ Traveller community? Why should we work with them?

The Gypsy/Traveller community in Derbyshire consists of Gypsies, Irish Travellers, Fairground families and other groups who are known as Travellers. The term 'Travellers' includes: Gypsies (of English, Welsh or Scottish origin); Irish Travellers; 'New Travellers'; Showmen (Fairground and Circus families); Bargees and other boat dwelling people. In addition, the Traveller Education Advisory and Support Team (TEAST) work with the Central and Eastern European Roma communities.

A short history of the Gypsy/Traveller community

(Extracts from *A better road*, an information booklet produced for healthcare and other professionals by the Derbyshire Gypsy Liaison Group and *Working towards inclusive practice* by Save the Children)

> *'The first authenticated records of Traditional Travellers' presence in Great Britain are in 1505 in Scotland. The first authenticated record in England is in 1514.*
>
> *Life was hard for Gypsy people in Europe before 1500. Laws were passed to expel Gypsies from Spain and Switzerland, and by 1650 most Gypsy people were slaves. In England, under Queen Elizabeth I, Gypsies were expelled along with all freed black slaves. Laws were passed condemning all Gypsies to death. When people*

were out of work, prices high and peasants were thrown off the land, it was the usual story of looking for someone to blame. Strangers make good scapegoats.

In York in 1596 magistrates made children watch while their parents were hanged just because they were Gypsies. After 1780 anti-Gypsy legislation was gradually repealed. Gypsy people became a useful source of cheap labour in the fields, as blacksmiths and entertainers. Gypsies survived on the margins of society.

After the mechanisation of farming, the lifestyle of Gypsies changed drastically. Not wanted for hop or strawberry picking or other traditional trades, the people found that they had to adapt. Again work was difficult to find for some families and the motorisation of families also changed travel patterns.

The mechanisation of traditional rural work started in the 1950s. The previous sources of livelihood did not provide sufficiently in the rural areas anymore. With industrialisation started migration from rural areas. The changes in society were also reflected in the Roma population. Many Gypsies moved from the rural areas to the cities and towns.

Over the past decades the material well-being of some Travellers has improved, but there are various issues that have been identified and need addressing, for example the unusually high infant mortality rate and the fact that the life expectancy of Traveller men is ten years less than

the national average and twelve years less for Traveller women.' (Derbyshire Gypsy Liaison Group, 2003, p.3.)
'Persecution is a constant theme in the experience of these communities. It is estimated that 250,000–600,000 Roma Gypsies died in the Nazi extermination camps. More recently, Roma communities have been persecuted in countries such as the Czech Republic, Slovakia, Poland, Bulgaria and Hungary. In the 1970s Czechoslovakia had a policy of compulsory sterilisation for Roma. Communism often gave way to violent nationalism and incidents of Roma being attacked by skinhead gangs are well documented. Much of this discrimination is institutional and even educated Roma young people find it almost impossible to find employment in their home country. In 1993 the new Czech and Slovakian republics rendered resident Gypsies stateless through new citizenship policies.' (Save the Children, 2006, pp.51–52.)

This history goes a long way to explaining why many Gypsy/ Travellers feel afraid of disclosing their culture (ascription).

'Even where the communities are not targeted in such ways, life is difficult. In Great Britain in the early 1990s, following panic over 'raves' and 'New Traveller' encampments, the 1968 Caravan Sites Act, which had placed a duty on local authorities in England and Wales to provide static sites for Gypsies, was revoked through the Criminal Justice and Public Order Act 1994, making it harder for the traditional Gypsy/Travellers to find somewhere to live. Many Gypsy/Travellers attempt to buy their own land but it is estimated that 90% of Gypsy

planning applications are refused (Wilson, M., 1997).
*In addition, widespread prejudice and racial
discrimination continue to persist in many areas. Racism
is commonplace and based on ignorance of the cultures
and traditions. As recently as 2003, 15-year-old Johnny
Delaney was beaten to death in a racist attack just for
being a Traveller.'* (Save the Children, 2006, pp.51–52.)

Since 2004, local authorities have had a legal requirement to
assess the accommodation needs of Gypsy/Travellers in their
areas and are now required to act to meet that need – but the
gap between need and supply remains large. Around two thirds
of Gypsy/Travellers reside on public or privately provided
permanent sites. The shortfall means that one third are forced to
camp on unauthorised sites. These Travellers are evicted and
moved from place to place, authority area to authority area. In
addition, of those Gypsy/Travellers who live in houses, many
would rather live in a trailer, but feel they have no choice
because of the shortage of sites and constant threat of evictions
if they are travelling.

Some Gypsy/Traveller families live in housing. The heritage
and culture make them who they are, not lifestyle choice. Being
a Gypsy/Traveller is a way of life and about much more than
living in a trailer. Their ethnicity is not lost through living in a
house. (Preceding two paragraphs adapted from Save the
Children, 2006.)

The culture of the Gypsy/Traveller community

'It is estimated that there are around 250,000 to 300,000
Gypsy/Travellers in Great Britain. Gypsy/Roma and Irish
Travellers are minority ethnic groups protected under the

*Race Relations Act 1976 as amended by the Race
Relations (Amendment) Act 2000; as proper nouns, the
words should therefore be capitalised like 'Jewish' or
'English'. Gypsies and Irish Travellers are in many ways
culturally different but have shared characteristics,
including a strong family unit with great value placed on
the care and socialisation of children and the care of the
elderly and infirm. They have a sense of pride and
resilience; entrepreneurial skills and occupational
adaptability; and a strict code of cleanliness with regard
to interior living spaces.' (Save the Children, 2006,
pp.51–52.)*

A Gypsy/Traveller woman's day revolves around household
chores. She takes pride in the appearance and cleanliness of her
home, inside and out. Looking after a family in a permanently
confined space is quite a challenge. She takes this role in her
family very seriously and is expected to do so.

The seasons play an important role for Gypsy/Traveller
menfolk in particular because of their work, which is most often
practical and outdoors. Families will often be more settled in
the autumn and winter, but around spring time and over the
summer they become much more mobile and will travel around
more.

Authorised residential sites are owned privately or by a local
authority. Sites are made up of a number of plots, usually
separated by fences, walls or other demarcation. A plot is an
area on which a family lives and will put their trailer(s) or mobile
home(s). Families frequently have two trailers, one to sleep in
and one to live in during the day. There will usually be a small
building with bathroom and basic kitchen facilities. A family will

rent a plot for an extended period of time and will often continue to do so while travelling. Some families rent plots in different parts of the country near other family members.

Authorised transit sites are owned privately or by a local authority. Sites are made up of a number of plots, but are often in an open area to allow flexible parking. There are usually electric hook-ups, water, shared toilets and showers. This all sounds very reasonable but in reality facilities are very often unusable and in bad repair because there is no one to take responsibility for upkeep and cleanliness. Families will use transit sites to stop off on their way to and from other sites, sometimes on their way to or from mainland Europe or Ireland for seasonal work. However, particularly if they are able to get a living locally, families will stay for extended periods of time. The shortage of places to pull on results in families using these sites as residential even though conditions and facilities are not appropriate for long-term stays.

In this unsettled and uncertain context it is not hard to see why families find difficulty in engaging with educational, health and other services for themselves and their children. Gypsy/Travellers have a higher infant mortality rate and lower life expectancy rate than the settled population of Great Britain. This is due in part to difficulty in accessing health services.

'Gypsy/Traveller families often remain excluded from many mainstream services and opportunities, particularly health and education services. An 'open door' policy in itself is not enough: an institution or system and the service it provides is in effect closed to anyone who does not know it and has no relationship with it.' (Save the Children, 2007, p.3.)

'Gypsies and Travellers have lower health status than the general population... Many of the health problems are related to the adverse environmental conditions in which families have to live, the difficulties they have in accessing sustained healthcare, and receiving up-to-date health advice and information, the stresses of forced moves, and the racism and discrimination they experience.' (University of Sheffield, 2004.)

Working with Gypsy/Traveller communities

It is important for professionals to see learners in the context of their family, culture and the community they live in, in order to relate to them and their cultures in a positive and enabling way. Traveller Education Services and Gypsy Liaison Groups are excellent providers of awareness-raising sessions for practitioners in a variety of settings. They can tailor presentations to particular groups and situations, including community settings, schools and children's centres. Save the Children's *Working towards inclusive practice* pack is also an excellent source of awareness-raising and training material (Save the Children, 2006).

Several distinct cultures are covered by the term 'Travellers' and so, as with any community, each site is different and demands a different approach to initiate the work. Each site is home to a different group of families, cultures, traditions and values; these varied communities reflect a variety of strengths, weaknesses and challenges and it is important to know and understand the groups that are represented.

'Traditional Travellers, both Romany and Irish, are reserved towards education since the school had been

seen as one means to assimilate Travellers into the society of the majority. The attitude towards education has changed during the last few years to a positive direction regarding the fact that the majority would like to see the children go to primary school.' (Derbyshire Gypsy Liaison Group, 2003, p.6.)

'How much a child learns in school, or how skilled and able he/she is, is not primarily important to Traveller parents. It is important for the child to have a safe and happy childhood. Traveller children have a lot of know-ledge of people and human nature from quite an early age. They receive teaching and wisdom from the adults and a child learns to live as a member of the community from birth' (Derbyshire Gypsy Liaison Group, 2003, p.8.)

A family session in progress

2 How ROWA! became involved

Read On – Write Away! (ROWA!) is an independent strategic literacy partnership which began in Derbyshire in 1997, with a range of national and local partners. ROWA! works to improve and celebrate the literacy and basic skills of people of all ages (0–99+), by working in and with local communities, with schools, with families, with young people, in the workplace and in prisons. ROWA! has found that its approach – a mixture of creativity, fun and celebration – really does engage those 'hard to reach' learners and encourage them back into learning.

One of ROWA!'s main strands is family learning. This is very often first steps back into learning for parents and carers. It is common for adults to participate in family learning when they perhaps wouldn't access learning for themselves – they will participate because they want to help their children. They come along to sessions and, as well as being supported to help their children, they can begin to address their own learning needs in a safe and supportive environment. Programmes have been developed for many different settings and communities.

In 2004, a multi-agency working group was set up to discuss the needs of a Gypsy/Traveller community on one site in north-east Derbyshire. The aim of the group was to bring a learning experience to a hard-to-reach community with low or no previous educational experience and no tradition of education either side of compulsory school age limits. The group was made up of the local SureStart manager, TEAST early years teacher, a member of the Early Years Social Inclusion team and a teacher from the local nursery school.

The Early Years Social Inclusion team had identified needs within this Gypsy/Traveller community and had access to a children's fund. The north-east Derbyshire site had been identified as having a lot of families with children under five, who did not access local toddler groups or pre-school provision. The TEAST team had good links already on this site but their role was solely advisory and there was no remit to work with the children under three and their families. Both these teams recognised the need to work with the parents within these families as well as the children, but both were constrained by their own performance targets and their awareness of the difficulty of engaging these parents in an educational project.

The SureStart Healthy Living Bus had been visiting the Gypsy/Traveller site with sessions for children and young people, offering crèche and play activities for small children and cooking activities for older children. Health checks and advice were also offered for adults and children. Twenty-four sessions were delivered on Saturday mornings from December 2003 to April 2005. The SureStart staff recognised a need to encourage the Gypsy/Traveller parents to improve their skills, to understand why education is important and to learn how to support their children.

A celebration event

The initial meetings of the working group outlined these proposals:

- Gypsy/Traveller network forum meetings to be held three times a year (the initial multi-agency group evolved to become the north-east Derbyshire Traveller network forum)
- Gypsy/Traveller mums to be encouraged to access the parent/ toddler group at the local school
- The SureStart Healthy Living Bus to visit the site regularly
- Books for Babies to be given out to children of eight months and over (in line with national Bookstart programme)
- Books for Toddlers to be given out to children of two years and over (in line with national Bookstart programme)
- ROWA! to be contacted about the development of 'play sacks'.

All of these agencies and activities were drawn together into The Derbyshire Traveller Family Learning Project.

The aims of the project are to engage with parents and develop their skills, develop children's skills and to increase access to quality nursery provision; to work with Gypsy/Traveller families to establish a learning culture; and to ensure that all children receive the best possible support during the early years.

So began ROWA!'s involvement with Gypsy/Traveller communities. Following on from the play sacks activities, ROWA! was given funding by Derbyshire's Early Years and Childcare Department to develop a family learning programme for the Gypsy /Traveller families. This was to be developed from its previous work within settled communities of hard-to-reach families.

3 Getting going: the partnership framework

ROWA! began work on the initial family learning pilot on the site in north-east Derbyshire. During this activity the staff leading the sessions began to develop relationships with other organisations working on site, particularly through the local Gypsy/Traveller network forum meetings.

Following the success of the initial programme, plans were in progress to replicate the project at a second site but in a different district of the county. In addition, we were already receiving requests for work at a third site.

Because of this sudden growth in the programme, we recognised the need for input at a strategic level. We needed management commitment to allow us to develop work with Gypsy/ Traveller families that was continuous and consistent rather than 'as and when we can'. Developing this was beneficial to all concerned – the families, the practitioners, and the managers.

Specifically, trust and understanding could be built on all sides, thereby facilitating the relationship and benefiting all. Within a managed framework, we could factor regular contacts and visits into our work plans and routines and more frequent contact allowed us to address needs and identify issues at an earlier stage, thereby preventing problems arising. By committing to the partnership and supporting frontline staff in the joined-up work, we were fulfilling our remit to deliver our service to Gypsy/ Travellers, widening participation within a deprived and marginalised community.

We proposed, therefore, to form a steering group for the project, peopled by strategic-level representatives from organisations and agencies who were involved with the Gypsy/Traveller families. The project co-ordinator, employed by ROWA! took the lead in forming, developing and facilitating this group.

Project steering group

The steering group was launched and continues to meet three times a year, working collaboratively to facilitate learning and development opportunities for Gypsy/Traveller families. New partners have joined since the initial meeting. The group seeks to ensure that Gypsy/Travellers have high priority in local plans

INSPIRATIONS

In Derbyshire, we are lucky enough to be able to work with an award-winning Gypsy/Traveller self-help group, the **Derbyshire Gypsy Liaison Group (DGLG)**. DGLG won the Queen's Golden Jubilee Award for Voluntary Work in 2003 and The Queen's Home Office Award in 2004 (in conjunction with Derbyshire Police for Innovative Police Training). They have also been held up as an example of good practice by the Department for Communities and Local Government (DCLG), for their inter-agency work.

and in the delivery of services. The formalised partnership of statutory and community groups enables the steering group to bid for funding to broaden and add value to mainstream services.

This joined-up approach also helps to ensure the best value from available services; joint working reduces costs for individual organisations and the outcomes and benefits are often increased. For example, an event may be organised involving three different organisations: each organisation provides one member of staff for the event, thereby meeting their individual targets, but with the added benefit of greater impact.

The Gypsy/Traveller community is represented on the steering group by the Derbyshire Gypsy Liaison Group. This is an essential element, ensuring that the community is an integral part of planning activity. If there is not a group running in your area, the National Federation of Gypsy Liaison Groups can offer helpful advice.

Action plan

The steering group produced an initial action plan with the following key priorities, which have remained the same to the present time. These are to:

- consult with Gypsy/Traveller families and partners
- improve links with education settings that Gypsy/Traveller children attend
- develop, strengthen and maintain partnerships
- link with other projects nationally, looking at best practice
- conduct action centred research and evaluation
- compile data and statistics.

Data and statistics

It was agreed that, because of the movement of Gypsy/Traveller families on and off the sites, the performance indicators would focus on the collection of data and information rather than specific achievement targets. This data and information, specified below, is crucial to inform partner organisations of need and this in turn informs the delivery of services; it also enables the impact of the project to be measured.

The key performance indicators are:

- education starting and finishing points: measuring the 'learning distance travelled' of adults and children
- attendance at sessions: frequency
- breakdown of attendance: gender, age, relationship, type of Gypsy/Traveller
- attendance in relation to eligible families on site (percentage)
- attendance at pre-school and school: eligible children and their siblings
- attitudes to education: feedback from education settings
- referrals to partner services
- case studies: qualitative information to be written by project staff.

Early partnership success

In 2005, the Derbyshire Traveller Family Learning Project was central to the success of Derbyshire County Council winning the highly prestigious 'SureStart Partners in Excellence Award for Integrated Care and Early Learning'. The award recognised that families on the Gypsy/Traveller site were at the heart of the planning, implementation, review and development of the project and that, through partnership with voluntary, statutory and private organisations, the project provided better access to health, education, sports, arts and play activities for the Gypsy/ Traveller community.

The work of the project and other projects involved with Gypsy/Traveller families in Derbyshire, feed into and draw from local strategic groups. *Appendix 1* outlines this relationship.

4 What happened in practice – the warts 'n' all!

One of the major advantages of this project was the ROWA! bus and driver. The bus is a converted double-decker with a learning space/IT suite upstairs and crèche/play/learning facilities for children downstairs. The driver's role involves more than driving the bus. He sorts out practical issues, diverts the attention of older children and young people who might otherwise disrupt the sessions, and helps to build relationships with the men on the sites.

Before starting the programme on a site, we use 'link people' – colleagues who already work with the families – to facilitate meetings with the site manager. Through these meetings we agree suitable days, times and a parking space for the bus, arrange distribution of coloured flyers to promote the sessions and inform all the residents about the programme. We also negotiate 'ground rules' with partners to ensure a consistent multi-agency approach. For example, it was crucial to support TEAST by not allowing school-age children to access the sessions during school hours. We could not create a diversion or alternative to school as this would undermine their work.

Early days
We began by visiting the families individually in their trailers and giving each of them a bag containing a book and a toy. We explained that the bus would be coming each week and described the sorts of activities that would be happening. But,

The ROWA bus on a residential site

more importantly, we played with the children in the trailers and modelled telling a story using the toy and book, crucially without reading the words just using the pictures as prompts – many of the parents told us at this stage that they couldn't read or write.

We added something to the bag each week to encourage attendance – sometimes a book, sometimes an activity, e.g. play-dough, crayons or glue. Two mums came on the bus 'just to have a quick look'; they stayed for a cup of coffee and a chat and the children played happily. The following week the children pestered their mums to take them on the bus again and gradually other parents and carers started to come along with their children too.

The first phase of sessions was very informal with mums and

INSPIRATIONS

J, J, M and H (mother, father, daughter, son) As a family they have all accessed the facilities on the bus and seem to enjoy coming on. M has grown in confidence during the project and now very willingly talks to all the staff on the bus and joins in all that is going on. H also enjoys the activities. Mum J has always been keen to come onto the bus when she can and shows interest in making activities for her children to do back in their trailer. Over the months that we have been on the site, J has become much more talkative to staff on the bus and there have been valuable informal conversations with the health worker on the bus. Dad J has also brought the children onto the bus on several occasions and has accessed the computers for himself.

other carers coming along for a change of scene, a coffee and a chat, knowing their children would be happy and that it didn't matter if they made a mess. These initial sessions were run as joint sessions with a number of activities provided for them to join in as they chose. Many parents requested childcare and we explained that this was not why we were there.

Over time we gradually added more structure to the sessions until we had the model we use today with both individual and joint sessions. Through activity and consultation, we built up trust and understanding; the project co-ordinator and other project staff became familiar and trusted faces. They were often asked for help and advice regarding many different aspects of life. They were able to signpost and make initial contacts to other services and in some instances act as advocates to help resolve issues for families. These aspects, although not part of the education/learning remit, were an extremely important part of the project.

> "L has been really helpful and I understand her. I don't like going to the doctor's as I don't understand what he's saying to me." (A parent)

Throughout this first phase we often had disruption from older children and teenagers on site. They wanted to access the bus and were bored. Some parents were upset that their older children were not allowed on the bus. It was very difficult as the young people clearly had needs. We worked with the site manager to address the issues and he spoke to some of the parents on our behalf, explaining that this project was for the very small children. We were also able to work with partners to provide a few sessions of appropriate activities for the older children, out of school hours, so that they wouldn't be left out completely. This approach seemed to work since throughout the following phases of delivery there was very little disruption.

Finding the right model

A particularly valuable aspect of our model of family learning for Traveller families is that we value what parents bring with them – their values, culture, life experience – and we also recognise the parents' roles as the children's most significant influence and teacher, as well as their importance in their child's growth and development. Very often, Gypsy/Traveller families feel that the establishment, schools etc., are trying to take over what they see as their role. We aim to consolidate and strengthen their role as parents, but also to highlight the skills their children will need to be able to participate in the world:

> The first part of each session offers separate activities for adults and children: play and learning activities for pre-school children and adult learning activities for parents/ carers. The Skills for Life (SfL) tutor works with the adults, using the computer and internet access on the ROWA! bus, to work on their own literacy skills and preparing activities to support their children's learning. The family learning teacher, supported by the crèche/ playworker, works with the children on play and learning activities that are linked to The Early Years Foundation Stage Strategy 0–5.

> During the second part of the session everyone comes together to join in with songs, stories, messy play and other activities that help meet planned learning objectives. We give families resources and activities to use at home where older siblings and other members of the family can also be involved. A typical session plan and evaluation example are included in *Appendix 2*.

Understandably, we have developed and evolved the delivery model for the sessions since the pilot project in 2004/05, responding to needs and to evaluation recommendations. In

INSPIRATIONS

> **B (male child)**
>
> B and his younger brother have accessed family sessions when they have been resident on site and whenever an adult has been available to accompany them. During the first programme of standard delivery, they made progress but it was quite limited (two Stepping Stones). However, during the second programme of intensive delivery, B made excellent progress (nine Stepping Stones). He enjoyed taking part in challenging activities and games and was well motivated. The fact that the bus was there on consecutive days helped, as he remembered things from the previous day and could build on his learning.

terms of patterns of delivery we have found the need to develop two different approaches: one for work on residential sites and another for work on transit sites:

> On residential sites, we use a model of working most closely allied to mainstream family learning. Using the ROWA! learning bus as a venue, we deliver sessions on authorised Gypsy/Traveller sites once a week in term time during the autumn and spring terms. Each session is typically two hours long, and planned and delivered by a family learning teacher, a crèche/playworker and an adult

SfL tutor. The summer term is not included in the programme because this is the time when the families are most likely to be moving around, although that is possible at any time of year. As well as working well for project staff and families alike, this model also allowed SureStart public health staff to offer a weekly service on site using the bus as a base and focal point.

Initially when we came to deliver sessions on the transit site, we replicated the above model, which was working well on residential sites. However, because many families were on site for only a couple of weeks at a time, they were only able to access one or two of the family sessions before moving on. To counteract this, we devised an intensive delivery model. We delivered the same two-hour sessions but as ten sessions within a four-week period, rather than once a week. This meant, for example, that a family staying for a fortnight would be able to access five sessions instead of just two. Children and adults also found it easier to build on their learning due to the shorter time lapse between sessions. This model does, however, create challenges from the point of view of staff availability.

5 Family learning

One of the strengths of family learning is that the variety and number of activities is only limited by the creativity of the tutor, teacher and learner. Because our funding has come from Derbyshire County Council's Early Years budget, the children's learning has been central to our project. The children's learning and experience is the starting point for all our planning and activity.

In our experience, the majority of Traveller children's play happens outside. This results in them being strong, fit and active (their bike riding skills are second to none!). Their imaginative and role-play skills are often well developed, as are their practical problem-solving skills. Conversely, their indoor play tends to be quite limited, with parents/carers resorting to DVDs and videos rather than construction, puzzles, games or creative and messy play that help to develop a broad range of skills. Because they live in a confined, clean and ordered space, providing a rich variety of play and early learning activities and the storage required for these, is quite a challenge for families. To complement these home-life and play experiences, we try to offer a range of activities that the children would not necessarily have the opportunity to enjoy at home. Young children who are given mark-making materials such as sand, play-dough and paint, and lots of opportunities to use felt tips, crayons, chalks, paper, old envelopes and cards, for example, become more skilled and confident writers than those who miss out on such experiences. Similarly. the earliest months and years are the most important of all for developing communication skills. By the age of five years, 95 per cent of children's spoken language has been acquired through talking, playing, and singing songs and rhymes. (Basic Skills Agency, 2005.)

Programme and session planning

We begin programme and session planning with the children's learning aims and objectives. From these, we devise a joint learning activity – one where the parent/carer works with their child towards a specific skill, ability or disposition. Once we have decided on a joint activity, we then work backwards and decide what experience, understanding and knowledge the adult and child will each need to enable them to complete the activity; these elements then become learning aims for the individual adult and child sessions (see example session plan and evaluation in *Appendix 2*).

The adult session

This is led by the SfL tutor and will include lots of informal discussion about the children, their characteristics, skills, abilities and their needs, both now and in the future, and about how the parents/carers can help support and encourage development and learning in their children, including making the most of everyday events, tasks, activities and items in the home environment. Adults will prepare for the joint activity by talking about its aims and purpose, making and preparing any materials and resources, practising playing any games and talking about differentiation and ways to develop the activity further. They will also plan and prepare a home activity. In addition, adults will talk about their own learning needs and work towards their own individual learning aims. The SfL tutor prepares activities relevant to the everyday lives, interests and needs of the parents/carers participating; for example, form-filling, letter-reading/writing, help with driving theory.

The children's session

A family learning teacher, with the support of a crèche/play worker, leads this session. We will generally start with a 'favourite activity', for example play-dough, while everyone arrives and settles down. Also available at this time are a few other toys including construction toys, cars and puzzles. We have found that if too many different activities are put out at the same time the children become very excited and find it hard to settle, moving too quickly from one activity to another. It is therefore better to have a few activities out to begin with and then bring out others as the session progresses.

During this time of free play, the teacher and crèche/play worker take every opportunity to engage the children in conversation, to teach colours and numbers and to help them to develop skills such as sharing and taking turns. Most of the children who attend are not used to any form of structure and during the weeks we slowly build in a structure and expectation of behaviour in the session. Later in each session we aim to engage the older children in a more focused activity, which might include a handwriting pattern sheet, a simple cutting and sticking activity or a game. This is often connected to what will happen in the joint session. We try to end the session by gathering the children together for a story and a time of singing.

It must be stressed that this is the ideal plan for each session. In reality, the session has to be very flexible depending on the children who are attending and the frame of mind that they are in. We have found ourselves suddenly using something that they have made to tell a story or to sing a song, or finding that they want to look at a story again and we can then encourage them to use it to make something out of play-dough.

The joint session

This is led by the family learning teacher. At the start of the session, the children show their parent/carer the things that they have made or done during the children's session, and the parents/carers are encouraged to give praise. This time might also include a story or a few songs. The teacher will then tell the children what they are going to be doing with their parent/carer during the session, before setting them off on the activity which their parents/ carers will have already discussed and prepared for in the adult session. During this time, we support the parents/carers and sometimes help look after any babies so parents can work with the older sibling. At the end of the session, we encourage everyone to help tidy up, we discuss and show what has been made and give any information about home activities or things to bring for the following week.

Themes

We have used a number of themes to help bring a focus to our programmes. Good examples of popular themes are: traditional stories, colours, and transport. Although it is good to have a theme to link sessions, it is best to keep individual sessions self-contained and not rely on previous sessions' activities for the success of a session. It can be disappointing when families don't bring items or haven't completed home activities. Similarly, it is likely that families will not attend every session. It is always important to be prepared for new families to join the programme with differentiated activities for both adults and children to ensure that sessions are accessible for all.

Best laid plans...

Taking everything into consideration, planning is essential. You need to have aims and objectives, a clear plan and focus. However, more often than not things do not go according to plan! Flexibility is the key, having a number of activities 'up your sleeve' to enable you to respond when a need arises.

In these situations children's needs and requirements are easier to meet as there are always lots of resources available. In contrast, the needs that adults can suddenly appear with can be extremely complex. The SfL tutor needs to always be prepared for a broad spectrum of learners who often arrive unexpectedly. On more than one occasion, an adult has come to a session asking, "Can you teach me to read and write, love? I'm here today then we're moving on tomorrow." There is just about time for a deep breath before you have to quickly decide what small thing you can teach them in the next hour that will make a difference for them. This is where contextual learning comes into its own. It is good to take time to have a conversation to identify one activity or issue that they are facing, for example, paying a bill, completing an insurance claim form, reading a letter or making an appointment with the doctor.

Thankfully this situation does not arise every week and there is often opportunity to plan and build learning at a reasonable pace. However, it is always essential to be prepared, in particular with reading and writing activities at pre-Entry levels.

Although it can be tempting to consider 'winging it', it is essential, and good practice, to have sound learning aims and

INSPIRATIONS

T and K (mother and daughter)

T had often been encouraged by the health visitor to bring K onto the bus but she always said that she was too busy. Towards the end of last year they both came onto the bus for a few sessions but often didn't stay long. During this term they have been to nearly all the sessions and in fact are often waiting for us to arrive and are the first onto the bus. At first K found it hard to be separated from her mum and T seemed a bit unsure about leaving her. However, by the end of the project K was very happy to be left and would quickly settle down to play, often with the play-dough. Over the weeks she also grew in confidence and began chatting with staff on the bus. During the first joint sessions that they attended, T didn't seem to really enjoy working with her daughter and did all the making herself, completing it as quickly as possible before leaving the bus to cook tea. This changed over the weeks and they began working together with T encouraging K to join in.

objectives even if they have to be changed or adapted as you go along. If you don't know where you're going you won't know when you've got there or even if you've made any progress. It can be extremely rewarding when you are able to help and

INSPIRATIONS

> ## R (female adult carer)
>
> R approached staff on the bus asking for help to read. She had not been able to attend school as a child as her family were very mobile. She told us she felt frustrated because she could not read or write. She was also concerned because she was not yet married and told project staff that 'if you are an Irish Traveller woman and not married, you don't have a life'. She went on to explain that as a single woman she was expected to stay on site and look after her sister's children and not allowed out socially. She brought two children on the bus just so that she could access learning for herself. The tutor worked with her using phonics to help her begin to read. After a couple of sessions she moved on, not returning to the site during the remainder of the programme.

encourage learners to take small but steady steps towards their goals. It is helpful to learn to be satisfied, and indeed excited, by small achievements – a change in an attitude or disposition, confidence and self esteem can be a huge step forward for many learners.

Timing

Gypsy/Traveller women prioritise their household duties. It

follows then that to take part in 'non-essential' activity, such as a family learning session, they will want to have completed their housework first. In our experience we have found that the best time to provide sessions is early afternoon after lunch and before the tea-time rush begins. We have also found that, if their men are around on site, the women are not as comfortable coming along to sessions, as they feel the expectation on them to be running the home. On several occasions when their men have arrived home unexpectedly, we have known women to leave sessions immediately to tend to their husbands' needs.

Because of the seasonal nature of the men's work, families tend to travel more in the summer months. This has an impact on family learning sessions. Therefore, we focus our delivery activity from September to April when the families are more settled and resident on site. Sometimes we have continued until May spring bank holiday if the families have stayed around longer than usual.

Venues

Site conditions and facilities vary enormously. Some sites have a permanent community facility that is used by a number of organisations to offer services to residents. This could be a prefabricated building, a relocatable building or caravan. Many sites have no such facility. For our project, the ROWA! learning bus has been an essential resource to deliver the family sessions. However, if a mobile facility is not available or site conditions prevent access, a similar outreach model could be considered to work with individual families in their own trailers on a one-to-one basis.

6 Personal perspectives

The following are some personal reflections from those involved in the project, including project staff, partners and learners.

Project staff

The enthusiasm and dedication of all the staff involved is central to the success of the model. Staff have faced very difficult and challenging situations positively and with professionalism. There follows some accounts of the work they have been involved in and how they perceive it.

ROWA! project co-ordinator

The project co-ordinator's role has been very broad, incorporating many elements: building, developing and maintaining relationships with partners, practitioners, site managers and Gypsy/ Traveller families; consulting families on an ongoing basis; planning and delivering activities and resources to improve the literacy, language and numeracy skills of adults and children; recruiting suitably skilled and experienced staff; building links with education settings and with other projects regionally and nationally to share good practice; and evaluating project activity.

All this preparation takes time – lots of time. However, the preparation has been crucial for the success of the project.

My background is in project management and administration but also in family learning as a practising SfL tutor. When my manager told me that we'd been asked to develop a family learning programme with Gypsy/Traveller families, I immediately said I'd give it a go. I had no experience or knowledge of the community or cultures and so set about finding out all I could.

It is widely recognised and well documented that the Gypsy/Traveller communities are isolated and suffer from social exclusion. This means the families lack the confidence to access local support services and fear that they will face prejudice from the wider communities in which they are located.

My concerns were around not causing offence by my lack of knowledge of the cultures, saying the wrong thing, doing the wrong thing, etc. My biggest concern was, and actually still is, something I constantly question myself on: what right do I have to intrude and perhaps disrupt the culture and way of life? I fear that there is always the possibility of upsetting a fine balance of gender roles.

Another concern came from my first visit to the site with a social inclusion worker. The first question from the families was 'are you a teacher?' It soon became apparent that their experience of teachers on the site was of Traveller Education Services, with a perception of enforcement – making the children go to school. TEAST are one of our closest partners but, initially, as far as the families were concerned, we tried to distance ourselves; we very consciously wanted to put across our less formal role, and our offer of pre-school fun, messy play, crafts and stories. We wanted to be a 'carrot'.

I have learned so much over the four years of the project to date. I've learned a great deal about Gypsy/Traveller cultures, about the individuals and families who have accessed the sessions and what it means to be a Gypsy/Traveller. I've also learned a great deal about myself, my own prejudices and assumptions and other weaknesses, but also my strengths and extents of perseverance. The work has taken me way beyond my comfort zone on many occasions. I've been insulted by individuals and badly bitten by a dog, but I've always come back for more because the satisfaction and reward of being able to build bridges and make a difference to families' lives outweighs any discomfort.

ROWA! family learning teacher

As a primary school teacher working in schools and, more recently as a supply teacher, I have worked with ROWA! for a number of years. This work has involved delivering a variety of family learning courses mostly in school settings. When asked if I would like to be involved with the Gypsy/Traveller work I felt that I knew about the session structure and, due to my previous work with ROWA!, was happy to work with adults and children. I had no previous experience working with Gypsy/Traveller communities and was unsure as to what it would be like, but I was keen to get involved.

At first I found the work was often quite frustrating as we had no idea of who and how many adults and children would attend each week, and not everyone would be there at the start of the session. As a supply teacher I thought that I was used to being flexible, but this was tested and I quickly learnt that although it was good to have a plan for the session, I had to be very flexible in the planning of activities and able to change things as we went along, depending on who turned up and their frame of mind.

It is a challenging environment to work in, though enjoyable, and I greatly value working as part of a regular team. Being clear about the boundaries that we are working with (e.g. the age of

INSPIRATIONS

B (female child)

When she first came onto the bus, B didn't really make any eye contact or conversation and we only had a few smiles. She found it hard to concentrate on any activity for any length of time and was always very quickly distracted. She struggled with even the simple structure of the sessions and found it difficult to share and play with the other children and would get cross, hit out and throw things. She really required one-to-one attention. However, as the weeks have gone by, she has settled into the sessions and now is eagerly waiting to come onto the bus each week. Her behaviour has improved and she now enjoys playing 'cooking' with the other children, looking at books and playing 'Snap'. She has become very chatty and always wants to tell us things. She came onto the bus without any knowledge of colours, numbers or counting but has made progress in learning these over the weeks. She enjoys looking at the books and is able to retell the stories in her own words using the pictures. She enjoys a joke. B is required to attend school in September and the project has given her a real help towards being able to manage that.

children, and that no child is allowed on the bus without an adult) and helping each other enforce these has been very important.

It can be emotional work, for example when you have a child who is longing to come onto the bus who should be in school, or whose adult doesn't want to come on, but experience has taught us that it is much better to stick with the boundaries, as to break them causes confusion and often difficulties in future weeks. It has also been important to have time after the sessions to reflect, debrief and encourage one another, especially if it has been a difficult session.

It has been very rewarding to see changes and development in the children, especially in those who have attended regularly, and to know of our part in encouraging them and their parents/carers into further learning.

Final advice – be very flexible and have play-dough! (Everyone loves it!)

Crèche/play worker

My main job is as a nursery nurse in a local nursery attached to a primary school. The nursery had been approached by ROWA! to provide a member of staff to work on the bus on a local Gypsy/Traveller site. I put my name forward.

I didn't know what to expect and was a bit nervous the first time I went. The other staff on the bus soon put me at ease. The first ten sessions went quite quickly. Over the time that I have worked on the project, one child and her progress stand out in particular. When she came on the bus the first week she would not talk or even make eye contact, wasn't interested in any of the activities and couldn't settle. Over the weeks we visited the site, she changed to having a much longer concentration span,

INSPIRATIONS

S (male child)
When S first came onto the bus he showed no eye contact or efforts to communicate and was generally fairly 'wild'. He couldn't settle or concentrate on any activity and we felt like we achieved something if we kept his attention on something for a few minutes. However, during the weeks that he has been attending we have noticed much change. He enjoys playing with the construction toys and play-dough and will now sit for quite a long time playing and making things. He can listen to instructions and is beginning to talk and communicate with simple words.

playing games and doing craft activities, re-telling stories and being happy to chat and talk about what she'd been doing. She seemed a totally different child. I felt quite sad when she moved on with her family but I know that is their way of life. I'm glad I got to know them and hope I helped them in some way like they have helped me to learn a small part of their culture.

I see some of the parents from the site at school and nursery and I feel comfortable to talk to them and ask them questions about their life whereas before I would not have felt comfortable about doing so. I have found out how different and how similar their life is to my own. They also know me and ask questions about me and about school and nursery.

The bus driver

I found the Travellers and Travellers' sites not as intimidating as I had thought. I found that engaging the males on site in conversation about vehicles was a good way to break down barriers. It also helped avoid problems and gain their trust, and with that they helped to control the behaviour of the children and teenagers. I enjoyed the insight into a different way of life.

Partners

TEAST Early Years specialist teacher

As the Early Years teacher with Derby and Derbyshire TEAST, one of my roles is to encourage Gypsy Roma Traveller (GRT) families to access quality pre-school education for their children. I used to regularly visit families in their homes and use play boxes to give young children experience in the six learning areas.

I wanted to demonstrate the benefits of play and liaise with settings and families. When I was approached by the ROWA! co-ordinator regarding a family learning project to work on sites with families I was very interested as I felt this could have a positive result for everybody involved. From the start there were very good inter-agency links as plans were discussed and TEAST was able to help with knowledge of the families and their culture.

ROWA! has now worked on several sites in Derbyshire and this has ensured that many children have experienced some quality pre-school sessions. A key feature in this type of work is flexibility and ROWA! has shown this when facing challenges and opportunities. When it was realised how mobile the community on the transit sites were, the co-ordinator arranged to visit a site every day over a specified period to provide intense input rather than the more usual weekly programme which had proved successful on other sites. She also contacted local settings, for

Crèche worker making dips with children on the ROWA bus

example nurseries and children's centres, and arranged for members of their staff to work on the project on sites. This greatly benefits the families when they come to attend those settings themselves and gives the setting staff valuable experience and links with the community.

My role has been to support this project in many ways, including help with planning, attending some sessions, discussing record-keeping and consulting families. I am delighted to report that on one of the sites that has had the ROWA! project, every three- and four-year-old is currently attending a nursery. This has enabled me to spend more time working strategically.

Public health practitioner

The aim of the public health practitioner (PHP) role in working with the Gypsy/Traveller community is to enable families to access health services and to promote healthy lifestyles without compromising cultural diversity.

My work with the community commenced about halfway through the family learning project. This was an advantage as fieldwork staff from the project had already established a good foundation for inter-agency working with the children and their families. The project has acted as a catalyst for joint service provision in achieving the five outcomes for children: Be Healthy, Stay Safe, Enjoy and Achieve, Make a Positive Contribution and Achieve Economic Well-being.

The ROWA! bus was on site during term time each week for a period of two hours, working with pre-school children and their parents/carers. It was during the second hour that the PHP would attend to offer health advice. As the parents became accustomed to this they began to access services and request support and advice on a range of health issues.

This method of working enabled the PHP to assess health needs of children and families in an unobtrusive way through observation of parent/child interaction during structured play activities. General health issues were addressed through group discussion, and often solutions to families' difficulties in accessing other mainstream services were identified. Parents sought home visits to discuss confidential health problems.

The overriding advantage, however, was that it was joint partnership working which offered a seamless, cohesive and comprehensive service. There was a shared philosophy, vision and agreed principles of working with children and families. A key advantage was that families had choice. They were able to access the services of the PHP at the point of need. Without the ROWA! bus as a central point of contact, this is more difficult.

Learners

Many parents/carers felt they got something out of the sessions, whether this was having time for themselves, or learning for themselves and their children.

'Coming on the bus gives us a break from housework.'

'It's a treat for a Gypsy child's mother to have an hour on their own.'

'I know my children are safe downstairs... I've really enjoyed having time on my own learning something for myself.'

'I've enjoyed seeing what the children do with the teacher. And it's helped me to do more at home with all mine.'

'She takes it all in when we're reading stories...she's ready for school now. I was wary of sending her to school but now I think she'll adapt.'

'Mine is asking to read stories and make stories up at bedtime and that's never happened before.'

Some resented the age limit for children accessing the bus:

'There's no sense it [the bus] being here if the kids aren't allowed on.'

7 Measuring impact

It is important to measure the impact of any programme. Programmes working with Gypsy/Traveller families are likely to involve a higher cost per learner than mainstream provision. Funders are therefore even more likely to require that impact and progress are measured to justify the extra expense. Measuring impact is also crucial to inform future practice and development of the programme.

This can be challenging, particularly with adults who are working at Entry level, whose attendance can be sporadic and who, by their very nature, move on.

Qualitative data can be used to effectively demonstrate impact, for example through consultation transcripts and case studies. However, this is even more effective when combined with quantitative data. We have gathered evidence in a number of ways.

Ascertaining changes in attitude to education

By collecting and analysing nursery and school attendance data for children participating in programmes and their older siblings, we have been able to determine any medium-/long-term changes to families' attitudes to school/learning. This evidence can be combined with qualitative information gathered from the settings the children attend and has the potential to be an ongoing tracking process. In addition, we have been able to collect and compare attendance data with that of children who haven't participated in the programme.

Starting and finishing points – children

In September 2007, the DfES (now Department for Children, Schools and Families – DCSF) launched the new Statutory Framework for the Early Years Foundation Stage (EYFS) to set the standards for learning, development and care for children from birth to five years. As part of the *Childcare Act 2006*, the Framework was given legal force from September 2008.

We have taken the first three points from each area of the EYFS profile to create a measurement tool. This not only helps us to plan activities that deliberately give the children opportunities and encourage them to progress in relation to the profile, but also helps us to record our experience of their progression. This information is valuable to share with parents and carers and can help motivate them to actively praise and encourage their children's development. This evidence can also be combined with qualitative information.

Starting and finishing points – adults

Measuring adults' progress is by nature much more intrusive and has to be taken very gently. Relationships and trust need to be built first before even attempting to establish a starting point. Our experienced SfL tutors have been able to build up an initial profile of an individual's skill levels. We found that pre-Entry initial assessment materials were not appropriate for this group – the scenarios and illustrations used do not reflect the Traveller community and their experiences – leading to the need to develop customised assessment materials. The diagnostic assessment has not been a problem at all, however; in fact adults have been quite motivated and enjoyed the challenge.

The progress we have seen in the adults has principally been in relation to attitudes, dispositions, participation and confidence. This progress can be collected and analysed qualitatively.

Consultation

Since the pilot programme began in 2004, there has been an ongoing consultation process. This has been informal but very valuable in the development of the programme. In addition to the week-by-week discussion, we have visited families individually on a termly basis to conduct a more structured 'interview' to talk about what they think and feel about the provision, their needs and what they would like to see. We have also visited families who have not participated in the programme for whatever reason. In future, we would like to develop a consultation tool for the children, to enable us to capture their voices and feelings about their time with us.

8 The successes

Over a period of months, relationships and trust developed between the project team and the Gypsy/Traveller families, and the big bus began to be a welcome presence on the sites. Families began to build the sessions into their routines and we helped open doors to other services for them, as other professionals were able to build relationships and offer services in a relaxed environment. The families regarded us as approachable and friendly, and found the sessions fun and stimulating. Gradually, the literacy, language and numeracy of the adults and children involved began to improve.

Children with family learning teacher

9 Checklist

This chapter summarises some of the considerations that need to be made when working with Gypsy/Traveller families.

Preparation

- What are the cultures of the Gypsy/Traveller families you are targeting? Take time to do some background research and think about the issues and tensions that may affect your project.
- What type of site are they living on (residential, transit, unauthorised roadside, housed)? How big is it? How many families? Is it privately or local authority owned? All of these factors will affect how you plan and arrange your provision.
- Is there a shared community space on the site? If so, can you make use of the facilities? If not, can you arrange a mobile unit or individual sessions in families' own trailers?
- How aware of Gypsy/Traveller cultures are the practitioners and other people working on the project? Do they, along with the majority of the population, have fears and misconceptions? Awareness-raising at an early stage can avoid misunderstandings later.
- What are the families' fears and misconceptions? Consult with them at an early stage and take on board their concerns. Remember, this is an ongoing process and there's always more to learn.
- Use people already working with the families as 'link people' to facilitate meetings with site managers.

- Take time to build relationships – with partner organisations, with education settings, with Gypsy/Traveller groups, with site managers and, most importantly, with the families.

Planning

- Plan your timetable around the learners' lives, for example, in terms of time of day (we found early afternoon best) and time of year (we found September to April best).
- Creatively explore funding streams to support and add value to programmes, particularly where mainstream funding is linked to accreditations and other targets, or is very short term.
- Think about how you are going to measure the impact of the programme. This can serve to highlight wider benefits and long-term savings, particularly in situations where relatively small numbers of participants equate to comparatively high costs per participant.
- Make sure you have good communication between partners, to ensure a joined-up, consistent approach and message.

Delivery

- Be flexible! Have a session plan, but be prepared to change it according to who attends, what their needs are and what opportunities might arise – have a number of activities 'up your sleeve'.
- Liaise and negotiate with partners and families to set secure and consistent boundaries concerning age and participation.
- Be patient, persevering and take a flexible multi-skilled approach to deal with challenges such as managing inconsistent attendance and fluctuating numbers.
- Continually review aims and objectives to keep focused on

what you are trying to achieve, but look at how you can strike the balance between what is requested and what you can offer.

- Make sure that children's activities are carefully differentiated, to ensure all children are stimulated, especially when participants are very different ages.
- Don't bring out too many different activities for the children at one time – have a few out to begin with and bring out others as the session progresses.
- For the children, gradually build in structure and expectations of behaviour over time.
- Take time to talk to the adults (even if they're only there for one session) to find out their immediate needs and how you might make a difference to them.
- Manage your own expectations – it can be frustrating when learners move on when they're just starting to make progress, but remember that small steps can make a big difference.

10 Session resources

The following organisations produce useful resources for planning and delivering provision to Gypsy/Traveller communities.

Avon Consortium Traveller Education Service
Tel: 01454 862 620
Charborough Road
Filton
Bristol
BS34 7RA
A wide variety of books and resource packs for children and young people.

Cambridgeshire Race Equality and Diversity Service
Team for Traveller Education
Tel: 01223 508 700
Books for adults and children.

Cheshire Consortium Traveller Education Service
Tel: 01606 814 331
Woodford Lodge Professional Centre
Woodford Lane West
Winsford
Cheshire
CW7 4EH
A variety of books and resources for children and young people.

Durham Ethnic Minority and Traveller Achievement Service
Tel: 01740 656 998
Broom Cottages Primary and Nursery School
Ferryhill
Co. Durham
DL17 8AN
Excellent quality books and photographic resources for adults and family learning.

Essex and Southend Consortium Traveller Education Service
Tel: 01376 340 360
Information and Publications Service
PO Box 47
Learning Services
Essex County Council
County Hall
Chelmsford
Essex
CM2 6WN
A wide variety of books and IT resources for adults and children.

Moving On Books
Tel: 01629 583 300
C/O Derbyshire Gypsy Liaison Group
Ernest Bailey Community Centre
New Street
Matlock
Derbyshire
DE4 3FE
Catalogue available of culturally specific books for adults and children, as well as history books, novels and children's books.

Save the Children
www.savethechildren.org.uk/earlyyears
A really good source of information including a DVD of a Gypsy/ Traveller family sharing their story.

The Gypsy Collection at the University of Liverpool
http://sca.lib.liv.ac.uk/collections/gypsy/intro.htm
Archive collection of resources including photographs and academic references.

West Midlands Consortium Education Service for Travelling Children (WMCESTC)
Tel: 01902 714 646
WMCESTC
The Graisley Centre
Pool Street
Wolverhampton
WV2 4NE
A wide variety of books and resources for schools and families.

11 Useful organisations, contacts, websites and publications

Organisations

Derbyshire Gypsy Liaison Group (DGLG)

www.dglg.org

Ernest Bailey Community Centre
New Street
Matlock
Derbyshire
DE4 3FE
Tel: 01629 583 300
E-mail: info@dglc.org

Friends, Families and Travellers (FFT)

www.gypsy-traveller.org

Community Base
113 Queens Road
Brighton
East Sussex
BN1 3XG
Tel: 01273 234 777
E-mail: fft@gypsy-traveller.org

National Association of Teachers of Travellers and other Professionals (NATT+)
www.natt.org.uk

National Federation of Gypsy Liaison Groups
www.nationalgypsytravellerfederation.org

NIACE (National Institute of Adult Continuing Education), including the former Basic Skills Agency
www.niace.org.uk

Renaissance House
20 Princess Road West
Leicester
LE1 6TP
Tel: 0116 204 4200/1
E-mail: enquiries@niace.org.uk

Ormiston Children and Families Trust
www.ormiston.org

Central Office
333 Felixstowe Road
Ipswich
IP3 9BU
Tel: 01473 724517
E-mail: enquiries@ormiston.org

Romany and Traveller Family History Society
www.rtfhs.org.uk

Publications

A Better Road
An information booklet for healthcare and other professionals
Derbyshire Gypsy Liaison Group
Ernest Bailey Community Centre
New Street
Matlock
Derbyshire
DE4 3FE
Tel: 01629 583300

Broadening Horizons: Education and Travelling Children
Naylor, S and Wild-Smith, K
Essex County Council Learning Services
Available from pubs@essexcc.gov.uk
Easily accessible background information based on the experience of practitioners in a variety of settings.

Early Years Outreach Practice
www.savethechildren.org.uk/earlyyears
Save the Children England Programme
1 Eastgate
Leeds
LS2 7LY

Raising the achievement of Gypsy, Roma and Traveller pupils (DVD)
Department for Children, Schools and Families
www.standards.dcsf.gov.uk
Tel: 0845 60 222 60
DCSF Publications
PO Box 5050
Sherwood Park
Annesley
Nottingham
NG15 0DJ

ROWA! Early Years Gypsy/Traveller Family Learning Project Evaluation Report 2005–2007
www.rowa.org.uk
Tel: 01629 585603
Read On – Write Away!
County Hall
Matlock
Derbyshire
DE4 3AG

The Read On – Write Away! Family Learning Pilot Project Evaluation Report 2005 – Yvonne Spare/Sheffield University
www.rowa.org.uk
Tel: 01629 585603
Read On – Write Away!
County Hall
Matlock
Derbyshire
DE4 3AG

Travellers' Times
www.travellerstimes.org.uk

Working Towards Inclusive Practice
www.savethechildren.org.uk/earlyyears
Save the Children England Programme
1 Eastgate
Leeds
LS2 7LY

12 Glossary and abbreviations

Authorised (site) – a site recognised and authorised by a local or district council that has sought permission and been approved by the local planning department. Unauthorised sites do not meet the above criteria.

DfES (Department for Education and Skills) – UK Government department responsible for schools and adult learning. In 2007, it separated into the Department for Children, Schools and Families (DCSF) and the Department for Innovation, Universities and Skills (DIUS).

DGLG (Derbyshire Gypsy Liaison Group) – a voluntary self-help association working in local, regional and national capacity.

Diagnostic assessment – a tool used in the adult sector to follow on from initial assessment, giving more accurate assessment of specific skills and competencies.

Differentiation – adapting a resource or activity for use with a different ability or age.

Eligible (family or child) – for the purpose of the Early Years family learning project a family with children aged zero to five.

EYFS (Early Years Foundation Stage) – the learning, development and welfare requirements of children aged zero to five.

Early Years Foundation Stage profile – DCSF's framework for capturing the learning and development of individual children.

Initial assessment – a tool used in the SfL sector to provide an initial guide to a learner's level of ability and a starting point for that learner.

PHP (public health practitioner) – role to promote healthy life styles and help families to access health services.

Qualitative (data or evidence) – information in narrative form, written or recorded, to provide evidence of activity or achievement.

Racism – prejudice or discrimination based on the belief that race is the primary factor determining human traits and abilities. Racism includes the belief that genetic or inherited differences produce the inherent superiority or inferiority of one race over another. Racist behaviour includes discrimination, mockery, abuse or aggression towards members of another race on the basis of such a belief.*

Residential (site) – where Gypsy/Traveller families live on a plot for extended periods of time.

Roma – because their language has similarities with Sanskrit, one theory is that Roma are descendants of the ancient warrior classes of northern India, particularly the Punjab, with the suggestion that they left their homes in the tenth century and travelled across Europe. There are several theories, but it is certain that there were various tribes/groups and the generic origin of English Gypsies, Central and East European Roma is likely to be the same.

ROWA! (Read On – Write Away!) – an independent strategic literacy partnership based in Derbyshire.

Six learning areas – these are:
- personal, social and emotional
- communication, language and literacy
- problem solving
- reasoning and numeracy
- knowledge and understanding of the world
- physical and creative.

SfL (Skills for Life) – formerly 'basic skills' including literacy, language and numeracy.

TEAST – Traveller Education Advisory and Support Team (Derby and Derbyshire).

Trailer – Gypsy/Traveller name for their caravan or mobile home.

Transit (site) – where Gypsy/Travellers pitch their trailers and live for short periods, a few days or weeks while travelling.

* Adapted from: www.adl.org/children_holocaust/more_resources.asp

13 Bibliography

Basic Skills Agency (2005) *Language and play: group leader's guide*, London: The Basic Skills Agency.

Derbyshire Gypsy Liaison Group (2003) *A better road: an information booklet for healthcare and other professionals*, Derbyshire: DGLG.

DCSF (2008) *Raising the achievement of Gypsy, Roma and Traveller pupils*, Nottingham: DCSF

Read On – Write Away! (2007) Early years Gypsy/Traveller family learning project evaluation report: September 2005 to March 2007, Derbyshire: ROWA!

Save the Children (2006) *Working towards inclusive practice: Gypsy/Roma and Traveller cultural awareness training and activities for early years settings*, London: Save the Children.

Save the Children (2007) *Early years outreach practice*, London: Save the Children.

Spare, Y. (2005) *The Read On – Write Away! Family Learning pilot project at the Corbriggs Traveller Site Derbyshire*, Sheffield: University of Sheffield.

University of Sheffield (2004) *The health status of Gypsies and Travellers in England*, Sheffield: University of Sheffield.

Wilson, M. and ACERT (1997) *Directory of planning policies for Gypsy site provisions in England*, Bristol: Policy Press.

Appendix 1:
Partnership structure

The work of this project, and other projects involved with Gypsy/Traveller families in Derbyshire, feed into and draw from local and strategic groups. The following diagram illustrates how the three groups fit together, their different functions, participants and aims.

Gypsy/Traveller network forum groups
Discuss and address ground-level needs, issues and services relating to an individual site

---

Project steering group
Works collaboratively to facilitate learning and development opportunities for Gypsy/Traveller families and to establish a learning culture. The group seeks to ensure Gypsy/Traveller families have high priority in local plans and delivery of services

Traveller issues working group
Addresses issues regarding the provision of sites, services and facilities, identifying gaps. Responds to legislation

Gypsy/Traveller forum groups

Each of the main Gypsy/Traveller sites in Derbyshire has a Traveller forum group. Members of the Gypsy/Traveller community are encouraged to attend and participate in the forum meetings alongside the operational staff and practitioners who, as part of their wider role, work with Gypsy/Traveller families. They discuss ideas, needs, issues, concerns and day to day activity.

The practitioners come from different areas, for example children's centre staff, health visitors, education, welfare and the police. Participation and access to events and services are often at the forefront of discussions. Relevant regional and county issues are also brought to the meeting.

The county and city Traveller issues working group

The concerns and issues considered by local groups inform the work of the Traveller issues working group. This group has representatives from specific departments within county, district and city councils. Like the steering group, it is a strategic level group but deals with separate issues; it looks at the provision of sites, services and facilities, identifying gaps and acting as a central contact point. District Housing Department representatives are key to the work of this group.

Appendix 2: Example session plan and evaluation

Date:	Venue:

Adults' learning objectives

- To think about and discuss name/initial recognition
- To make name/initial recognition activities for joint session and home activity
- To participate in form-filling activities

Children's learning objectives

- To link some sounds to letters – focus on initial/name
- To build relationships through gesture and talk
- To explore different media and respond to a variety of sensory experiences

Joint learning objectives

- To support children to link sounds to letters and objects
- To support children to recognise initial letter sound
- To support children to recognise initial letter shape

Child activity	Adult activity	Joint activity
• Time of free play with a variety of toys and activities • During play focus on initial sounds of objects • Objects box with items that begin with the same sound as children's names • Each child selects objects that begin with their sound to show parents/carers	• Time of discussion about process of name recognition • Talk about opportunities at home • Talk about letter sounds and names – focus on sounds • Make children's initial templates for joint collage activity • Discuss aims of joint activity	• Time together to show initial letter objects from child session • Songs • Story • Parent and child create collage of child's initial letter shape • Look at home activity – folding book to collect letters and pictures of objects

- Older children letter and name pattern sheets
- Story and children's choice of songs

- Look at everyday forms
- Share ideas and issues, look for similarities in layout and questions
- Practise filling in forms

Evaluation	Date:	Venue:
Child activity	**Adult activity**	**Joint activity**
• Who attended • What they did • What went well • What didn't go so well • Things to remember for next session	• Who attended • What they did • What went well • What didn't go so well • Things to remember for next session	• Who attended • What they did • What went well • What didn't go so well • Things to remember for next session

Playing 'Kim's Game' on the ROWA bus